Japanese Mochi Recipe Cookbook

Delightful Sweet Japanese Mochi Recipes to Satisfy Your Sweet Tooth!

BY

Rachael Rayner

License Notes

No part of this Book can be reproduced in any form or by any means including print, electronic, scanning or photocopying unless prior permission is granted by the author.

All ideas, suggestions and guidelines mentioned here are written for informative purposes. While the author has taken every possible step to ensure accuracy, all readers are advised to follow information at their own risk. The author cannot be held responsible for personal and/or commercial damages in case of misinterpreting and misunderstanding any part of this Book

Table of Contents

Introduction

This collection of Japanese Mochi recipes are all simple and easy to prepare. My hopes that these recipes will help to guide you into the world of preparing Japanese Mochi. Enjoy preparing this special treat for your loved ones in a simple fashion. You will be using the modern method of Mochi preparation that will not need any special equipment, but instead, you can use the utensils that you have in your home kitchen.

One of the great delights in preparing Japanese Mochi is that there is a wide range of assorted fillings that you can use. You will get to choose from a wide selection of fillings such as cream cheese, raspberry jam filling, butter filling, chocolate filling, etc. The traditional Mochi was served just by itself, this being the most basic of preparation of Japanese Mochi. My collection of Japanese Mochi recipes will be a great start or introduction for you into mastering the art of creating Japanese Mochi for your friends and loved ones hopefully for many years to come!

Japanese Sweet Mochi
Recipe Collection

1. Sweet Mochi

This Sweet Mochi recipe uses green tea ice cream to add to the flavor of the Mochi.!

Preparation time: 2 minutes

Total Cook time: 4 minutes

Servings: 10

Ingredients:

- potato starch to use for dusting
- 1 cup of water
- 1 cup Mochiko
- vanilla ice cream
- ¼ cup of sugar

Directions:

1. In a mixing bowl that is microwave safe, combine the sugar, water, and Mochiko.

2. Place the mixture in the microwave for 4 minutes or until the Mochi is set.

3. Dust the surface with the potato starch.

4. Carefully, roll out your Mochi and divide it into portions.

5. Scoop ice cream into each part and then enclose.

6. Serve the sweet dish immediately and Enjoy!

2. Simple Mochi

This Sweet Mochi recipe is one of the oldest Japanese sweet dish recipes.

Preparation time: 2 minutes

Total Cook time: 4 minutes

Servings: 10

Ingredients:

- Vanilla ice cream
- Potato starch to use for dusting
- ¼ cup of sugar
- 1 cup of water
- 1 cup of Mochiko

Directions:

1. In a mixing bowl, combine the sugar, water, and Mochiko.

2. Place bowl in the microwave for 4 minutes or until the Mochi is completely set.

3. Dust the surface with the potato starch.

4. Roll out your Mochi and divide it up into portions.

5. Add some ice cream into the individual parts and then enclose.

6. Serve immediately and enjoy!

3. Chocolate Mochi Bars

Trying to find something to snack on? Look no further as these chocolate Mochi bars make for a perfect snack!

Preparation time: 15 minutes

Total Cook time: 30 minutes

Servings: 20

Ingredients:

- 2 cups of Mochiko
- ½ a stick of butter
- 1 teaspoon vanilla extract
- 1 can evaporated milk
- 1 egg
- ½ teaspoon baking soda
- 1 cup white sugar
- ½ cup of chocolate chips

Directions:

1. Preheat your oven to 350° Fahrenheit.

2. Mix the sugar, Mochiko, and baking powder in a bowl.

3. In another bowl mix the evaporated milk, egg, and vanilla extract.

4. Melt the butter along with the chocolate chips, then add the egg mixture. Mix well.

5. Add the Mochiko mixture to your wet ingredients.

6. Add batter to a baking dish and bake for 30 minutes.

7. Serve and Enjoy!

4. Microwave Mochi with Chocolate Chips

With only a few ingredients, this Mochi recipe is extremely simple to prepare.

Preparation time: 15 minutes

Total Cook time: 4 minutes

Servings: 25

Ingredients:

- 1 ½ cups of Mochiko
- ¼ cup of sugar
- 25 chocolate chips
- 1 cup of white sugar
- 1 ½ cups of water
- 2 drops of vinegar
- potato starch for dusting
- ¼ teaspoon salt

Directions:

1. To make the rice cake, mix the white sugar, Mochiko, water, and vinegar. Microwave for 4 minutes or until it sets.

2. Roll your Mochi onto the potato starch, salt, and sugar until coated.

3. Cut into pieces and then shape into balls while placing a chocolate chip into each ball.

4. Serve and Enjoy!

5. Broiled Mochi with Nori Seaweed

This is a unique preparation of Mochi as it is boiled and makes use of more novel ingredients such as Nori.

Preparation time: 17 minutes

Total Cook time: 7 minutes

Servings: 8

Ingredients:

- 1 sheet of Nori
- ½ cup of soy sauce
- 8 Frozen Mochi squares

Directions:

1. Preheat your oven to 450° Fahrenheit.

2. Cut your Mochi into squares and dip into the soy sauce.

3. Set the dipped Mochi squares on a baking sheet and bake for 5 minutes.

4. Add the seaweed strips to a saucepan over medium heat, and warm for 2 minutes. Cool them.

5. Wrap each of your Mochi with a piece of seaweed.

6. Serve and Enjoy!

6. Dark Chocolate Mochi Truffles

These Mochi truffles are a real favorite that is enjoyed primarily by kids.

Preparation time: 30 minutes

Total Cook time: 10 minutes

Servings: 16

Ingredients:

- ½ cup of cocoa powder
- 250 grams of dark chocolate
- ½ cup of heavy cream
- 1 teaspoon vanilla extract
- 2 tablespoons unsalted butter
- 1 ½ cups of cornflour
- 2/3 cup of water
- ¼ cup of sugar
- 2 cups of rice flour

Directions:

1. To prepare the ganache, begin by melting the dark chocolate and the butter in a double boiler for 5 minutes.

2. Stir in the cream along with the vanilla extract.

3. Let cool.

4. Shape your ganache into balls and then coat them with cocoa powder.

5. Dust your surface with some corn starch.

6. To prepare your Mochi, mix the sugar, rice flour, and water and heat for 4 minutes in the microwave or until they have set.

7. Roll out your Mochi and divide into portions.

8. Enclose your ganache balls and cover.

9. Serve and Enjoy!

7. Chocolate Glazed Mochi Doughnuts

This lovely sweet Japanese inspired treat is made using rice cake and the richness of the chocolate.

Preparation time: 30 minutes

Total Cook time: 10 minutes

Servings: 10 servings

Ingredients:

- 2 cups of Mochiko
- ¼ cup of sugar
- 1 egg
- ½ cup of milk
- 3 tablespoons milk
- 9 tablespoons of butter, melted
- 1 ½ tablespoons baking powder
- 1 teaspoon vanilla extract
- warm water to use for kneading
- 1/3 cup of coconut milk
- 12 ounces dark chocolate
- 2 cups of powdered sugar
- olive oil for frying doughnuts

Directions:

1. Mix the milk with ¼ of the Mochiko. Place in the microwave for 4 minutes or until they are set.

2. In a second mixing bowl, add the remainder of the Mochiko, along with egg, milk, sugar, baking powder, and vanilla extract. Mix well.

3. Add the cooled microwaved Mochiko to the uncooked Mochiko mixture. Knead the dough well.

4. Roll out your dough and dust it with flour, then cut it into doughnut shapes.

5. Heat you're oil over medium heat in a pan. Add the doughnuts to heated oil and heat until golden in color for about 5 minutes.

6. In a small saucepan melt the dark chocolate over high heat, then add the coconut milk and stir. Remove from heat and cool.

7. Drizzle the cooled chocolate over the doughnuts. Sprinkle doughnuts with powdered sugar.

8. Serve and Enjoy!

8. Warabi Mochi Recipe

Within this recipe is included two of Japan's most common ingredients; they are known as Warabi Mochiko and Kinako.

Preparation time: 30 minutes

Total Cook time: 5 minutes

Servings: 24

Ingredients:

- 2 cups of Warabi Mochiko
- 1 cup of Kinako
- ½ cup of sugar
- 1 cup of lukewarm water

Directions:

1. In a mixing bowl, add the Warabi Mochiko and water, then mix until smooth. Add the sugar and mix until well combined.

2. On a baking sheet, sprinkle the Kinako onto it.

3. Heat your Warabi Mochiko mixture in a saucepan over medium-high heat for about 5 minutes or until it becomes thick.

4. Pour your Warabi Mochiko mixture on top of the Kinako and allow it to set.

5. Pour more Kinako on top.

6. Slice into squares after it has completely cooled and set using a sharp knife.

7. Serve and Enjoy!

9. Pumpkin Mochi

In this recipe with the addition of pumpkin makes these Japanese sweets a bit different.

Preparation time: 10 minutes

Total Cook time: 60 minutes

Servings: 12

Ingredients:

- 2 ½ cups Mochiko
- 4 eggs
- 2 teaspoons baking powder
- 2 teaspoons vanilla extract
- 1 cup butter, melted
- 1 can of pumpkin puree
- 2 cups white sugar

Directions:

1. Preheat your oven to 350° Fahrenheit.

2. In a large bowl mix the Mochiko with sugar and baking powder. Set aside.

3. In a separate bowl, mix the pumpkin puree, eggs, condensed milk, vanilla extract, and melted butter.

4. Mix together all your ingredients, and pout into Mochiko mixture and combine.

5. Pour your batter into a baking dish and place in the oven and bake for 60 minutes.

6. Allow cooling before serving.

7. Serve and Enjoy!

10. Guamanian Mochi

Guamanian Mochi is most commonly eaten in Hawaii. It's sweet, soft, chewy and sticky, with a delicious taste you are sure to enjoy!

Preparation time: 10 minutes

Total Cook time: 30 minutes

Servings: 48

Ingredients:

- 2 cups of Mochiko
- 1 tablespoon baking soda
- ¼ cup of butter, melted
- 1 can coconut milk
- 1 teaspoon vanilla extract
- 2 eggs
- 1 ¾ cups of white sugar
- 1 can of evaporated milk

Directions:

1. Preheat your oven to 350° Fahrenheit.

2. In a bowl mix your Mochiko with white sugar and the baking soda.

3. In another mixing bowl, beat the eggs with coconut milk, evaporated milk, melted butter, and vanilla extract. Mix well.

4. Mix the Mochiko mixture with egg mixture.

5. Pour your batter into a baking dish and bake in your oven for 30 minutes. Cool before serving.

6. Serve and Enjoy!

11. Chilled Strawberry Soup with Chocolate Strawberry Rice Balls

This is a wonderfully divine tasting recipe that will have you going for seconds!

Preparation time: 12 minutes

Total Cook time: 20 minutes

Servings: 2

Ingredients:

- 3 tablespoons of sugar
- 1 cup of strawberry puree
- 3 tablespoons of water
- juice of 1 lemon
- 1/3 cup of plain yogurt
- 3 tablespoons seltzer water
- ½ cup of rice flour
- 3 tablespoons of powdered sugar
- 20 chocolate chips
- 5 tablespoons strawberry puree

Directions:

1. In a saucepan heat your sugar and water until it is completely dissolved.

2. In your blender add the strawberry puree, seltzer water, yogurt, and lemon juice. Blend.

3. Add the melted sugar and blend again.

4. Place in your fridge to chill.

5. To prepare your chocolate sweet rice balls, boil water in a pan.

6. In a bowl, combine your rice flour, powdered sugar, and strawberry puree until it forms a sticky dough. Slowly, knead your dough mix, until it is no longer sticky.

7. Roll balls from the dough and add chocolate chips into the balls.

8. Add balls to boiling water and cook until the balls for 20 minutes or until they float to the top of the water.

9. Add the balls into your chilled soup and serve cold.

10. Serve and Enjoy!

12. Strawberry Cream Cheese Mochi

This Strawberry Cream Cheese Mochi is a wonderful recipe to serve at parties!

Preparation time: 12 minutes

Total Cook time: 20 minutes

Servings: 2 dozen

Ingredients:

- 2 cups of Mochiko
- 1 teaspoon almond extract
- 2 tablespoons of powdered sugar
- 4-ounces of cream cheese
- 2 ¾ cups of water
- 1 cup of sugar
- 1 teaspoon Katakuirko
- ½ cup of strawberries

Directions:

1. Mix the powdered sugar, almond extract, and cream cheese in your blender. Place in your fridge.

2. In a pan boil your water and add in the sugar. Cook until sugar is dissolved.

3. Add your Mochiko to water at ¼ cup at a time.

4. Add in your almond extract.

5. Dust the surface with your Karauirko and turn the Mochiko onto it.

6. Roll your Mochiko until flat. Divide.

7. Add the cream cheese filling to each Mochiko and enclose. Garnish with strawberries.

8. Serve and Enjoy!

13. Strawberry Daifuku Mochi

This Mochi recipe is a delightful treat that is filled with tasty bits of sweet strawberries!

Preparation time: 10 minutes

Total Cook time: 20 minutes

Servings: 10

Ingredients:

- 10 strawberries
- 1 cup of rice flour
- ½ a cup of sugar
- 1 ½ cups of cold water
- plenty of potato starch for dusting the surface
- 1 ½ cups of Anko

Directions:

1. Rinse and dry your strawberries.

2. Coat your strawberries with the Anko paste and cover them. Place in your fridge.

3. In a bowl, add the rice flour, sugar, and water. Mix to dissolve.

4. Place in the microwave for 2 minutes or until it is cooked.

5. Dust the surface with plenty of potato starch and pour your rice flour mixture on top of it, so it does not stick.

6. Roll your dough, then use a pastry cutter to cut your dough into 10 pieces.

7. Remove your coated strawberries from the fridge and place one strawberry in each piece of dough then enclose. Allow them to set.

8. Serve and Enjoy!

14. Strawberry Mochi

This Mochi recipe is delicious as it uses strawberry juice that gives it good flavor!

Preparation time: 5 minutes

Total Cook time: 2 minutes

Servings: 2

Ingredients:

- ¼ cup of cane sugar
- 1 cup of rice flour
- 2/3 cups of water
- 12 tablespoons of strawberry jam
- 3 tablespoons strawberry juice
- ½ cup of cornstarch

Directions:

1. In a mixing bowl, combine the strawberry juice, water, rice flour, and sugar. Mix ingredients to form a thick paste.

2. Cook the mixture in your microwave for 2 minutes.

3. When done, allow the dough to cool then flatten it.

4. Dust the surface with cornstarch and make 12 Mochi from the dough.

5. Add about 1 tablespoon of strawberry jam onto each Mochi then enclose it.

6. Serve and Enjoy!

15. Chocolate Butter Mochi

This is a delightful flavored chocolate butter Mochi recipe that is easy to prepare!

Preparation time: 10 minutes

Total Cook time: 45 minutes

Servings: 7

Ingredients:

- 2 cups of sugar
- 16 ounces of Mochiko
- 2 eggs
- 2 teaspoons vanilla extract
- 1 can of coconut milk
- 1 can of evaporated milk
- 1 ½ cups of chocolate chips
- ½ cup of butter
- 1 teaspoon of baking soda
- 3 tablespoons cocoa powder

Directions:

1. Preheat your oven to 350° Fahrenheit.

2. Mix your Mochiko, baking soda, and sugar in a mixing bowl then set aside.

3. Melt the chocolate chips and butter in a saucepan over low heat.

4. In a different bowl, mix the coconut milk, eggs, vanilla extract, and evaporated milk. Beat mixture until well combined.

5. Add the dry ingredients and then mix until well combined.

6. Pour your mixture into a prepared baking dish and bake for 40 minutes. Serve and Enjoy!

16. Tasty Chocolate Mochi Cake

This chocolate Mochi cake is full of chocolate flavor and has a beautifully rich and gooey taste that you are sure to love!

Preparation time: 15 minutes

Total Cook time: 60 minutes

Servings: 16

Ingredients:

- 1 cup of Mochiko
- 1 cup of sugar
- 1 egg
- 1 teaspoon vanilla extract
- 1 can evaporated milk
- ½ cup chocolate
- ¼ cup of butter
- 1 ½ teaspoon baking soda

Directions:

1. Preheat your oven to 350° Fahrenheit.

2. In a mixing bowl, combine the baking soda, sugar, and Mochiko.

3. In a small saucepan melt the butter and chocolate.

4. Beat the vanilla extract, evaporated milk, and egg using a beater.

5. Add the dry ingredients (Mochiko, baking soda, and sugar) and mix well.

6. Add you're batter into a baking dish and bake for 60 minutes. Cool before serving.

7. Serve and Enjoy!

17. Chocolate Mochi Mug Cake

This recipe is great for those late-night cravings, and it is quick and easy to prepare!

Preparation time: 5 minutes

Total Cook time: 1 minute

Servings: 1 mug cake

Ingredients:

- 2 tablespoons of sweet rice flour
- 2 tablespoons non-fat milk
- ½ tablespoon of cocoa powder
- 1 tablespoon of sugar
- ½ tablespoon of vegetable oil

Directions:

1. In a mug, add your sweet rice flour, baking powder, sugar, and cocoa powder.

2. Mix your wet ingredients until the batter is smooth.

3. Place batter in the microwave for 1 minute.

4. Serve and Enjoy!

18. Chocolate Mochi Snack Cake

Enjoy this Japanese recipe of chocolate Mochi snack cake that has a lovely soft and chewy texture!

Preparation time: 5 minutes

Total Cook time: 45 minutes

Servings: 7

Ingredients:

- 2 cups of rice flour
- 2 eggs
- 2 cups of white sugar
- 24-ounces of evaporated milk
- 1 cup of chocolate chips
- ½ cup unsalted butter
- 1 tablespoon baking soda
- 2 teaspoons vanilla extract

Directions

1. Preheat your oven to 350° Fahrenheit.

2. In a mixing bowl, combine the baking soda, rice flour, and sugar, then set aside.

3. Melt your chocolate chips and butter over low heat in a pan.

4. In another bowl, beat the vanilla extract, evaporated milk, and eggs into the chocolate mixture and mix well.

5. Add the dry ingredients (sugar, flour, and baking soda), and mix until well combined.

6. Bake the batter in a baking dish for 40 minutes. Let the dish cool.

7. Serve and Enjoy!

19. Chocolate Mochi

Enjoy this yummy traditional Hawaiian Japanese recipe for chocolate Mochi!

Preparation time: 10 minutes

Total Cook time: 45 minutes

Servings: 10

Ingredients:

- 2 cups of Mochiko
- 2 cups of white sugar
- 2 eggs
- 2 teaspoons vanilla extract
- ½ cup melted margarine
- 2 cans of evaporated milk
- 1 cup of semi-sweet chocolate chips
- 1 tablespoon baking soda

Directions:

1. In a mixing bowl, mix the sugar, Mochiko, and baking soda.

2. Melt the chocolate chips and margarine in a saucepan over low heat. Add your eggs, milk and vanilla extract and mix until well combined.

3. Pour smooth mixture into a baking dish and place in a preheated oven at 350° Fahrenheit for about 45 minutes.

4. Serve and Enjoy!

20. Chi Chi Dango Mochi

Delight your tastebuds with this traditional Japanese recipe of chi chi dango Mochi!

Preparation time: 15 minutes

Total Cook time: 1 hour

Servings: 36

Ingredients:

- 1 pound of Mochiko
- 1 ½ cups potato starch
- ¼ teaspoon of red food color
- 1 teaspoon vanilla extract
- 1 teaspoon baking powder
- 2 cups of water
- 1 can coconut milk
- 2 ½ cups white sugar

Directions:

1. Preheat your oven to 350° Fahrenheit.

2. Mix the sugar, rice flour, and baking powder in a bowl.

3. In another bowl, mix the coconut milk, water, vanilla, and red food coloring.

4. Mix the coconut milk mixture and the flour mixture.

5. Pour the ingredients into a baking dish.

6. Bake your mixture in preheated oven for 1 hour, then allow cooling.

7. Dust surface with potato starch and place the Mochi on the potato starch and slice into pieces.

8. Serve and Enjoy!

21. Ono Butter Mochi

This recipe for Mochi is prepared with butter and coconut with a base of rice. A great treat to serve at tropical parties!

Preparation time: 15 minutes

Total Cook time: 1 hour

Servings: 12

Ingredients:

- 1 pound of Mochiko
- 2 ½ cups of white sugar
- 5 eggs
- ½ cup melted butter
- 1 teaspoon vanilla extract
- 1 cup of sweetened flaked coconut
- 3 cups of milk
- 1 teaspoon baking powder

Directions:

1. Preheat your oven to 350° Fahrenheit.

2. Take a mixing bowl, and add the eggs, vanilla extract, milk, and whisk together.

3. Combine in another bowl, the rice flour, baking powder, and sugar.

4. Mix your dry and wet ingredients until well combined.

5. Mix the butter and flaked coconut.

6. Add ingredients into a baking dish and bake in preheated oven for an hour. Cut into squares.

7. Serve and Enjoy!

22. Strawberry Mochi with Red Bean

Enjoy the unique flavor of this Strawberry Mochi with the red bean!

Preparation time: 10 minutes

Total Cook time: 2 minutes

Servings: 6

Ingredients:

- ½ a cup plus 1 tablespoon of red bean paste
- 2 tablespoons of sugar
- ½ a cup of water
- potato starch or cornstarch—to roll
- ¾ cup of rice flour
- 6 large strawberries

Directions:

1. Divide your red bean paste into 6 even portions.

2. Coat each of the strawberries with red bean paste. Store in the fridge.

3. Dust the surface of cutting board with cornstarch or potato starch.

4. To prepare the Mochiko, mix your rice flour, sugar, and water.

5. Microwave this mixture for 2 minutes or more until set.

6. Pour the Mochiko onto the dusted surface of cutting board and roll it out and divide it into 6 equal portions.

7. Remove the coated strawberries from the fridge and place a strawberry onto each Mochiko and enclose.

8. Serve and Enjoy!

23. Honey Mochi

The honey Mochi is an excellent source of fiber, so make sure to add this recipe to your list!

Preparation time: 10 minutes

Total Cook time: 3 minutes

Servings: 24

Ingredients:

- 2 tablespoons honey
- 2 cups of water
- 2 cups Adzuki beans
- 2 tablespoons brown sugar
- 2 tablespoons sugar
- 2 tablespoons salt
- 2 cups of rice flour

Directions:

1. Pour rice flour into mixing bowl.

2. Mix in your sugar, salt, Adzuki beans, and water.

3. Add the honey and brown sugar.

4. Add the water into the honey mix while stirring.

5. Make 24 balls out of dough and place them on a plate.

6. Heat them in your microwave for 3 minutes.

7. Serve and Enjoy!

24. Sesame Mochi

This Sesame Mochi recipe is a tasty way to get your protein!

Preparation time: 10 minutes

Total Cook time: 10 minutes

Servings: 24

Ingredients:

- 2 tablespoons black sesame
- 2 tablespoons of food coloring
- 2 cups Mochi pieces
- 2 tablespoons sugar
- 2 cups of Nerikiri dough

Directions:

1. Place your Mochi pieces in a mixing bowl.

2. Mix the Nerikiri dough, sugar, black sesame, and food coloring.

3. Make 24 balls out of dough. Heat a pan.

4. Cook balls in the pan for 10 minutes on low heat.

5. Shape the Mochi when ready.

6. Serve and Enjoy!

25. Kinako Mochi

Kinako Mochi is a beautiful recipe that is rich in vitamin A, C, and E, and will help to keep your body healthy and functioning properly!

Preparation time: 10 minutes

Total Cook time: 10 minutes

Servings: 24

Ingredients:

- 2 cups of Kinako
- 2 cups of walnuts
- 2 tablespoons oil
- a dash of salt
- 2 cups of rice flour
- 2 cups of Glutinous rice flour
- 2 tablespoons warm water

Directions:

1. Add your rice flour into a bowl.

2. Mix the glutinous rice flour with the warm water.

3. Make a dough out of it.

4. Add your Kinako and salt.

5. Add your oil into a pan and heat over low.

6. Add small portions of the mixture into the pan, cook for 10 minutes on both sides.

7. When done sprinkle Mochi with walnuts.

8. Serve and Enjoy!

Conclusion

Firstly, I would like to conclude by extending my thanks and appreciation to all of the readers that invested their time and money in my cookbook! I am genuinely grateful that you chose my Japanese Mochi recipe collection out of all the books out there. I am more than happy in knowing that my readers are enjoying my work; this makes my efforts well worth it!

My goal with this book was to introduce you to preparing Japanese Mochi using an easy and straightforward approach. I am confident that in no time you will be using these recipes to help you to master the art of Japanese Mochi. Keep in mind that it is essential that the rice flour is not too dry or it will be hard to consume. You do not want it to be too sticky, or it will stick to your hands. Having the perfect rice flour will undoubtedly lead you towards a successful Mochi!

You can help countless other readers that can benefit from your opinions and insight by leaving a review of this book on Amazon. I truly hope that you and your loved ones will

gain many years of enjoying preparing and most of all –
eating this delightful collection of Japanese Mochi recipes!

Author's Afterthoughts

THANK YOU

Thanks ever so much to each of my cherished readers for investing the time to read this book!

I know you could have picked from many other books, but you chose this one. So, a big thanks for downloading this book and reading all the way to the end.

If you enjoyed this book or received value from it, I'd like to ask you for a favor. Please take a few minutes to post an honest and heartfelt review on Amazon.com. Your support does make a difference and helps to benefit other people.

Thanks for your Reviews!

Rachael Rayner

About the Author

Rachael Rayner

Are you tired of cooking the same types of dishes over and over again? As a mother of not one, but two sets of twins, preparing meals became very challenging, very early on. Not only was it difficult to get enough time in the kitchen to prepare anything other than fried eggs, but I was constantly trying to please 4 little hungry mouths under 5 years old. Of course I would not trade my angels for anything in the world, but I had just about given up on cooking, when I had a genius idea one afternoon while I was napping beside one of my sons. I am so happy and proud to tell you that since then, my kitchen has become my sanctuary and my children have become my helpers. I have transformed my meal preparation, my grocery shopping habits, and my cooking style. I am Racheal Rayner, and I am proud to tell you that I am no longer the boring mom sous-chef people avoid. I am the house in our neighborhood where every kid (and parent) wants to come for dinner.

I was raised Jewish in a very traditional household, and I was not allowed in the kitchen that much. My mother cooked the same recipes day in day out, and salt and pepper were probably the extent of the seasonings we were able to detect in the dishes she made. We did not even know any better until we moved out of the house. My husband, Frank is a foodie. I thought I was too, until I met him. I mean I love food, but who doesn't right? He revolutionized my knowledge about cooking. He used to take over in the kitchen, because after all, we were a modern couple and both of us worked full time jobs. He prepared chilies, soups, chicken casseroles—one more delicious than the last. When I got pregnant with my first set of twins and had to stay home on bed rest, I took over the kitchen and it was a disaster. I tried so hard to find the right ingredients and recipes to make the dishes taste something close to my husband's. However, I hated follow recipes. You don't tell a pregnant woman that her food tastes bad, so Frank and I reluctantly ate the dishes I prepared on week days. Fortunately, he was the weekend chef.

After the birth of my first set of twins, I was too busy to even attempt to cook. Sure, I prepared thousands of bottles of milk and purees, but Frank and I ended up eating take out 4 days out of 5. Then, no break for this mom, I gave birth to my second set of twins only 19 months later! I knew that now it was not just about Frank and I anymore, but it was about these little ones for whom I wanted to cook healthy meals, and I had to learn how to cook.

One afternoon in March, when I got up from that power nap with my boys, I had figured out what I needed to do to improve my cooking skills and stop torturing my family with my bland dishes. I had to let go of everything I had learned, tasted, or seen from my childhood and start over. I spent a week organizing my kitchen, and I equipped myself a new blender. I also got some fun shaped cookie cutters, a rolling pin, wooden spatulas, mixing bowls, fruit cutters, and plenty of plastic storage containers. I was ready.

My oldest twins, Isabella and Sophia are now teenagers, and love to cook with their Mom when they are not too busy talking on the phone. My youngest twins Erick and John, are now 10 years old and so helpful in the kitchen, especially when it's time to make cookies.

Let me start sharing my tips, recipes, and shopping suggestions with you ladies and gentlemen. I did not reinvent the wheel here but I did make my kitchen my own, started storing my favorite baking ingredients, and visiting the fresh produce market more often. I have mastered the principles of slow cooking and chopping veggies ahead of time. I have even embraced the involvement of my little ones in the kitchen with me.

I never want to hear you say that you are too busy to cook some delicious and healthy dishes, because BUSY, is my middle name.

Made in the USA
San Bernardino, CA
12 March 2020

65580662R00051